MODERN ICONS

KISS

Acknowledgments

With very grateful thanks to Philip Dodd, Lucinda Hawksley,
Helen Johnson, Morse Modaberi and to John Stickland,
Gary Stickland and the staff of the National Sound Archive
for their help in the research of this book.

Sylvie Simmons has been obsessed with both rock and writing since well before the age of consent. One morning in '75 she woke up to discover that you could put them together, and got a job as pop writer on a teen magazine. Since then she has spent seven years in the States working on *Sounds*, *Kerrang* and *Creem*, among others, as well as co-hosting a radio show. Sylvie now writes for *Mojo*, *Kerrang*, *Top* and the European edition of *Rolling Stone*.

Modern Icons conceived and developed
for and with Virgin Publishing Ltd by Flame Tree Publishing,
a part of The Foundry Creative Media Company Limited,
The Long House, Antrobus Road, Chiswick, London W4 5HY.

ISBN 0-312-17941-3

Library of Congress Cataloging-in-Publication Data available on request

First published in the United Kingdom in 1997 by Virgin Publishing Ltd.

First U.S. edition

10 9 8 7 6 5 4 3 2 1

KISS

Introduction by Sylvie Simmons

St. Martin's Press
New York

CONTENTS

CONTENTS

INTRODUCTION

There was a hold-up at a Kiss concert once – out in the Midwest a pimply youth waved a gun at the box office and yelled 'Hand them over'. Not the takings. What he wanted was three tickets to a sold-out show for himself and two fellow footsoldiers in what they called the Kiss Army. This was back in the Seventies, when Kiss were *it*, the number one group in the States, the biggest, the loudest. The band whose elaborate make-up, outrageous costumes and blood-spitting, fire-bombing, ear-splitting shows made mothers weep, critics mock, and the Moral Majority – hell, before there even *was* a Moral Majority – beat their breasts and burn their records. Which sold, of course, in their millions to pimply youths, with or without guns, across the United States.

Back in the days before Generation X, before arcades and computer games, for that matter before computers, Kiss was the pagan religion for America's adolescents. Kids shoehorned into black spandex would raid their mothers' Max Factor, steal their sisters' shoes, stuff an avocado down the front of their trousers and troop in their tens of thousands to sports arenas to watch bassist Gene Simmons – dragon-man – strut about in thigh-high scaly platforms, jiggle his leather batwings, shove out his tongue (rumoured to have been given a snip-job on the gristle underneath to make it stick out further), cough fire and drool blood over the front row; vocalist Paul

Stanley – cartoon matinee idol, a glitter rock star over half his face – pout and strut like a Page Three girl; guitarist Ace Frehley – the spaceman who always looked like he'd got too high – totter about on his platforms and play his six-stringed phallus; and drummer Peter Criss – whiskered cat man – sit at his drums and, well, basically look like a drummer made up to look like a cat.

The music? I suppose you'd call it Metal Bubblegum – a perfect fusion of Pop (songwriters Simmons and Stanley grew up on The Beatles) and Heavy Metal (they were big Led Zeppelin fans), played at a volume as loud as their outfits. They'd sing about the usual subjects – sex, more sex, sometimes heart-tugging sex, more often dirty sex,

with the occasional diversion into drinking and partying all night long – chuck in some solos, set off some bombs, smash up their instruments and leave the entire stage smouldering into dust. As rock encyclopedist Lillian Roxon put it, they were Walt Disney on acid. Not forgetting testosterone. The stuff that male teen fantasies are made of. Songs like 'Christine Sixteen', 'Fits Like

A Glove', 'Room Service'. You get the idea. As Paul Stanley told me, back in their heyday, 'We never sing about the state of the world because we *are* the world. We write about fucking.' And sex sells.

From those of you who came up in the Eighties, I can understand the collective 'So what?': Motley Crue had harder drugs, tighter spandex, better-looking groupies; W.A.S.P spat raw meat at the crowd, *their* bassist wore a flame-throwing codpiece; and so on and so on. In the Eighties cock-rock ruled. Ecologists sobbed at the hairspray-induced hole in the ozone layer and the number of whales it took to keep all the bands in face-paint.

But let's put this in context. When Kiss formed it was the early Seventies – post-hippy, post-pop innocence, the cusp of a period that would bring a mind-boggling growth in the music industry. All rock'n'roll movements are about reaction, and the seriousness that fell upon rock and pop music at the end of the previous decade – the drug casualties, the murder at Altamont, the self-important supergroups, Progressive Rock

with its classical pretensions, the bland middle-of-the-rock bands like the Doobie Brothers and Atlanta Rhythm Section with their unshowy jeans-and-T-shirt shows – spawned in reaction the silliness and flash of Glam Rock. The year that Paul Stanley met Gene Simmons, David Bowie released 'Ziggy Stardust' – and Simmons saw Slade in concert (the platform shoes and the spelling of the Slade-esque hit 'Rock And Roll All Nite' are a bit of a give-away).

So the stage had been set. But the timing was crucial. At almost the exact moment that Simmons, Stanley, Frehley and Criss made their debut at a club in Queens, New York, rock'n'roll/pop music – invented, along with the concept of the 'teenager', in the late Fifties – had just left its adolescence. Those who'd grown up in that first brash, egotistical, anything-goes era were now, like Kiss, forming bands themselves, with a new audience eager to embrace them.

Kiss were arguably the first big rock band for the second generation of American teenagers. There was no other band like them. Okay, AC/DC were playing brain-shatteringly loud, so were The Stooges and MC5, Alice Cooper did a hell of a show, and Bowie, Sweet and Gary Glitter knew their way around the cosmetic counters. But Metal and Punk then were pretty small-time in the States. And Glam, as Alice's band name affirms, was linked with androgyny: fine for weak-wristed, lily-livered Brits, but not for red-blooded, veins-in-the-teeth, all-American boys. Kiss took the volume and the searing guitars from Punk and Metal, avoiding its ghetto by writing singalong anthems. And they helped themselves to Glam's pose and look and attitude, sidestepping its androgyny by becoming cartoons, comic-book superheroes, übermenschen. Kiss's trademark was never to be seen, off-stage or on, out of costume or make-up.

In 1973, Bruce Springsteen was making his debut, Genesis was on the road, and the biggest-selling albums were Mike Oldfield's synthesised, self-important 'Tubular Bells' and Pink Floyd's concept album, 'Dark Side Of The Moon', when Paul Stanley, who used to sing in Top 40 covers bands, and Gene Simmons, a schoolteacher, were in

the process of evolving from part-time group, Wicked Lester, into Kiss. They tracked down Criss from a small ad in *Rolling Stone* ('Drummer willing to do anything to make it') and Frehley from an ad in *The Village Voice*. By the year's end they had a management deal with Bill Aucoin, and, on New Year's Eve, a spot on the bill with Blue Oyster Cult, Iggy Pop and (whatever happened to?) Teenage Lust. A week later, they were the first act signed to Neil Bogart's Casablanca label; a month later,

they'd released their debut album, 'Kiss', promoted in the States with, what else?, a nationwide kissing contest. And the band went out on the road – seven nights a week, 18 months straight, only taking a week or two off to go back in the studio. November the same year saw the release of their second album. Def Leppard would have died.

You can only imagine what it must have been like for all those sweaty-palmed, hormonal young Americans seeing the band in some small hall for the first time, or opening for any band that dared have them – four fantasy creatures seven-foot tall in their massive black platform-boots, looking like Marvel Comic versions of Japanese kabuki theatre actors, if they'd known what kabuki actors looked like. From the beginning, the look, the show, the package, was paramount. Gene Simmons may have the (self-confessed) mind of a slut, but it was coupled with the brains of a businessman. To get a really big slice of the ever-increasing music industry pie, they'd have to come up with something new.

'We sat around and said, let's be bigger, let's be different, let's be the band we never saw,' Paul Stanley told me early on. 'I remember a lot of bands that I saw that really knocked me out visually didn't do a lot for me musically and vice versa. What we wanted to do was

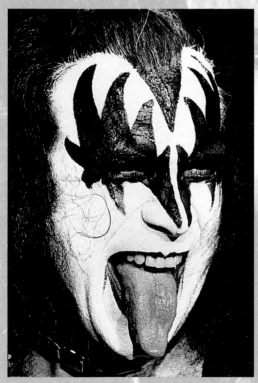

bring the two together and have the kind of music we were doing fit the kind of show we were doing – have a recognisable image. I think the bands that were always the most appealing were ones you could look at and say "those four guys belong together. One guy doesn't look like Rip Van Winkle and one like Mick Jagger – it looks like a group".' Added Gene Simmons, 'When we first started it was like you had to be out of your minds to put on make-up when everybody else looked like The Little River Band . . . but though whatever it is that I was onstage with Kiss – the demon form – may not be classically defined as attractive, shit, there were certainly enough girls that wanted to fuck that thing!'

Kiss, in a word, worked. The critics dismissed them, then loathed them. But by their fourth album, 'Alive!', in 1975, they were stars; by their sixth, in 1976, 'Destroyer', they were *megastars*. And by 1977 – the year of 'Saturday Night Fever' and The Sex Pistols – they were a one-band industry. There were Kiss lunchpails for sale, Kiss school satchels, Kiss pinball machines for the rich kids, Kiss pens and pencils for the financially-challenged. They were the first band to be immortalised in a Marvel comic book: Kiss fighting alongside fellow superheroes Spiderman and The Hulk. The band were millionaires. There seemed nothing too daring or egotistical for them: in 1978, all four released debut solo albums on the same day. And still no one had the foggiest what they looked like.

But the Seventies had to end. As the new decade rolled around, drummer Peter Criss did the unthinkable. He took off his make-up and showed his naked face on American TV. It looked somewhere between Christopher Cross and Father Christmas. He planned to launch a solo career, revealing that his musical love was not scorching Heavy Metal, in fact, but middle-of-the-road pop.

And, when you stopped to think about it, Kiss seemed to be mellowing out too. Their second post-Criss album, '(Music From)

The Elder', was – for crying out loud! – a *concept album* and a pretty naff one at that and didn't even go gold. And their over-the-top look appeared modified, more like the cuddly little monster toys your gran might buy for Christmas than the larger-than-life lumps of outrage and excess that gave your mum hysterics. And a second defection took place in 1982, when Ace Frehley left. Vinnie Vincent was the first of a long line of replacements.

However the biggest shock was to come a year later. There had been rumours for some time that the band would take off their make-up – some said it was an act of desperation, others an act of maturity. Loyal fans – and their loyalty had been tested of late – were torn between a desire to see what their heroes looked like, and horror that they might turn out to be the spitting image of Air Supply or Peter Criss or both. But there they all were, in September 1983, after a big promotional build-up, on the new music video station MTV, about to reveal all.

Who can say why something works and something else doesn't? By all accounts, one look at Simmons and Stanley *sans* face-paint, stripped of all mystique, possessed of dodgy haircuts and the looks that only a decade of decadent living can bring, should have sent the fans screaming to the younger, cuter, MTV-friendly New Wave of Metal bands. But the Kiss Army rallied behind its de-camouflaged leaders and 'Lick It Up', their first New-Dawn album, shot

up the American chart. The British one too, nestling at a respectable Number 7. Its follow-up, 'Animalize', restored their platinum status. The next couple of years saw Simmons cashing in on his naturally villainous looks by accepting a number of 'baddie' movie roles, and making the most of his business skills by launching Simmons Records. But their hit singles were ballads; Paul Stanley wrote one of them with the unforgivable

Michael Bolton. And there were some who thought that Kiss, essentially reduced to Paul and Gene plus whoever, wasn't so much a band any more as a two-man money-generating machine.

During the Eighties, Kiss's brand of flash, brash stadium cock-rock became bigger than ever and spawned a thousand imitators, but by the Nineties they were being referred to in terms of past-tense glory. Though acknowledged as an influence, they didn't seem to have the sense of cool attached to them that other influential bands like, say, Aerosmith or Judas Priest had. The Nineties was the era of Grunge

and Alternative – a reaction against the superficiality, excess and ego of the previous ten years. The new rock bands took a more introspective approach, reflecting on the woes of society and what-am-I-doing-here angst, rather than the size of their penises or a woman's ability to crush a beercan between her breasts.

So, bye-bye Kiss? Not quite yet. This was also the era of the Tribute Album. Any band worth their salt had had their songs covered by a collection of the popular new bands. Eventually they'd have got around to making a Kiss tribute album, but Simmons, astute as ever, made sure of it (and guaranteed control) by organising one himself. You'd be surprised at the people who wanted to appear – forty-two acts, at one point, from R&B-ers Stevie Wonder and Lenny Kravitz, to country and western star Garth Brookes, from old-style Metalheads like Anthrax to new-style Metalheads like Nine Inch Nails, plus Extreme, the Lemonheads, Faith No More and the rest.

And that wasn't the end of it. In 1996, Gene Simmons and Paul Stanley pulled out their make-up bags, tugged on their platform boots, tracked down Ace Frehley and Peter Criss and announced a massive, major reunion tour – the old costumes, the old pyrotechnics, the Dragon, the Matinee Idol, the Spaceman and the Cat. And it was a smash. Forget holding up the box office, people *killed* for tickets, among them the critics who'd slagged them in the past and the new bands who'd hid their Kiss albums at the back of the collection . . . as well as, apparently, half the population of the world. The merchandise on sale at the events was mind-boggling; the money Kiss made was extraordinary.

Kiss were no longer just a rock band. Kiss were *icons*. A band old enough to carbon date, a band that formed at the start of the Seventies, set the template for the Eighties, made a comeback in the navel-gazing Nineties and could still, on a good day, stomp the crap out of just about every American Metal band born of woman, couldn't be anything *but* iconic.

SYLVIE SIMMONS

KISS AND MAKE UP

. . . .

Kiss set out their intentions from their very first public gigs in January 1973. Booked into a club in Queens, NY – the venue changed its name from the Popcorn club to the Coventry on their opening night – they hit the stage already sporting make-up, some impromptu daubs that would evolve into the trademark characters they jealously protected and brilliantly exploited. Sadly, the audience for that first performance was only a handful of people: Gene Simmons's girlfriend, a couple of pals and the club barman, but they were witness to the birth of a band that already had very clear ideas about what it was going to deliver and how it was going to market itself. Although photos in the first press kit they prepared (self-confidence and self-publicity were talents they were never short of) showed the four members of the band with no make-up, over the next few months they developed the concept as a means of making them stand out from the crowd, a device to get them that extra edge of attention. Whether they realised it or not, they had stumbled, in pre-MTV, pre-promo video days, on the marketing potential of a highly visual image. From the mid-Seventies to the Kiss conventions of the Eighties and Nineties, Kiss fans could declare their allegiance by painstakingly copying Peter Criss's cats whiskers or Paul Stanley's single star. As Kissmania became a corporate industry in its own right, American magazines offered rewards to anyone who was

able to snatch a photograph of the four out of character. And if being hunted down by paparazzi eager to make a quick buck wasn't bad enough, Kiss also found that their image, although delivering spectacular commercial returns, gave their critics a severe attack of spleen. Coming off the back of the androgynous poses of Bolan, Ziggy Stardust and the New York Dolls, and the horror movie games of Alice Cooper, the serious music press saw Kiss as the butt-end of glam rock. If they had to resort to ridiculous face-painting, surely they were simply trying to hide their complete lack of talent? Consequently they received unprecedented amounts of journalistic vitriol. But it made little difference – their fans were hooked.

They're a good band.
All these guys need is a gimmick.

Alice Cooper,
at the Casablanca/Kiss launch party, 1974

*Gene Simmons and Paul
Stanley were the driving
force behind Kiss. Their
previous musical excursions
had not indicated a great
deal of promise, although
their first collaboration, a
band called Wicked Lester,
recorded an album for
Epic Records; it was never
released. Simmons and
Stanley regrouped, and
began to grope their way
towards a clearer vision of
the sound, the feel, the
personality and the look
of their next venture.*

In 1972 there was only
one impressive band in
New York at the time and
that was the New York Dolls.
Gene Simmons, *Billboard*, 1989

Kiss are a 1970's band for all those who claim there aren't any, and as if the name wasn't enough to put you on your guard they turn out to be New Yorkers as representative of that city as Vanilla Fudge or the Velvet Underground.

Max Bell, *NME*, 1975

We've often been accused of being pretentious, but in actuality our concept of what we're doing is an effort to shy away from pretentiousness.

Paul Stanley, *Melody Maker*, 1975

When we put Kiss together, we didn't really have a clue who should be in it, or even what we should call it, but we knew what the sound was going to be. Ace and Peter were chosen because they fitted that sound.

Gene Simmons

*They took the flamboyant groove of the glam rock era to new
extremes, but in the early days Kiss had a few false starts:
Gene Simmons described the look on their first poster as
'football players trying to look like the New York Dolls'.
Aggressively macho, they needed to find an image which
steered away from suggestive bisexuality. By July 1973, six
months after their first appearance on stage, the individual
designs for their make-up had been fixed, although the stack-
heeled, shoulder-padded costumes were still some way away.*

The band that first knocked me out was the Beatles. Up until
then, one wasn't aware of the visual presence a group could have.
And that concept knocked me out, especially the fact that there
was no front man and each member was a quarter of the whole.
Gene Simmons, *Melody Maker*, 1975

If make-up could come through on a record player,
Kiss would have a huge hit.
Jet Black, The Stranglers, 1977

People ask us who our role models were, but none of them were
musical. After we figured out the costumes and staging, we just kept
taking it a little further. One night, we just started putting make-up
on. It was all very nonchalant, like 'OK, it's time to put make-up on'.
Gene Simmons

I used to go to parties and flaunt the rock star rule, but now that I am one, I can't. I'm losing the real Peter Criss somewhere and it scares me.
Peter Criss, *Rolling Stone*, 1977

I think black leather is very tough and exciting. I'd much prefer something macho rather than coming on in pink satin.
Paul Stanley, *Melody Maker*, 1975

29

Eventually the make-up came off, but not for a decade. An issue of People magazine in August 1980 had run a feature on the band that included make-up-free shots, but it was another three years before Kiss finally removed the painted faces from their live act and public appearances. Record sales had been declining, particularly in the States, so they settled on exposure as a shock strategy. It was a muted shock: after so long, the faces they revealed were remarkably unremarkable. The Kiss Army rallied behind them though, and together they marched back to platinum sales.

We'd been doing it for ten years. We wrote the book on it. After ten years you want to be able to part your hair on the other side if you want to. We started that because it was a way of making our personalities larger, saying 'This is who we are'.

Paul Stanley, *Sounds*, 1984

The make-up is just the icing on the cake. You can add all the sugar coating you want, but if it doesn't taste good, it isn't going to make any difference. Ten feet out into the audience, you can't see the make-up anyway. It's the people under the make-up that matter.

Gene Simmons, *Melody Maker*, 1983

I'm so used to seeing myself with make-up that I had to look in the mirror to make sure it wasn't me.

Paul Stanley, on seeing a picture of 'himself' that was actually Mike Corby of The Babys

LARGER THAN LIFE

Having established the four fantasy characters as a key weapon in their attack on the unsuspecting youth of middle America, Kiss then brought in additional heavy guns to boost their stage show. At a time when the stagecraft of rock'n'roll was stuck in something of a rut, they created an on-stage experience that was rivalled only by Pink Floyd's in the progressive rock arena. But where the Floyd looked to link their explosions into the dynamics of their music, Kiss let rip with an arsenal of pyrotechnics that produced a fearsome onslaught. By 1975 their stage equipment included a battery of explosive flashes, oversized blowtorches, drumsticks that exploded and guitars that launched rockets. Gene Simmons had also, bar a few nights of singed hair and flesh, mastered the trick of fire-breathing. His mentor, Amaze-O the Magician, had been brought in by Neil Bogart, the head of their record company Casablanca. Bogart saw eye to eye with the band on the spectacle, and needed no persuading to get behind the move towards bigger and bolder stage effects. Casablanca Records were renowned within the business for the scale of their promotions, the lavishness of their parties and the hedonism of their workday lifestyle – legend had it that mid-afternoon a beautiful girl would tour the offices taking the staff's daily drug requests. Between them Kiss and Bogart created Kissland on stage: amid the explosions and against the backdrop of

wall-to-wall amps and speakers, banging out the decibels, the four band members could act out their roles. There was Gene Simmons, the lusty, licentious Demon, his supernatural tongue poking forth at every opportunity; Paul Stanley, the Star Child; Ace Frehley, a seriously psychedelic space cadet; and Peter Criss, the Cheshire Cat high up on his drum riser. It was pure theatrical spectacle.

We all have various personalities. On stage we let the fantasy come through. I believe in pulling on a show, if people pay to see you they expect you to be larger than life.
Gene Simmons, *NME*, 1975

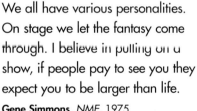

The Kiss publicity machine let its imagination run loose with each of the band's characters, inventing knockabout fantastical biographies. Simmons played up the macabre aspects of a bloodthirsty vampire: 'he joyfully exudes the evil he feels is part of all of us'. Stanley claimed he was the reincarnation of a medieval prince, brought back to life to devote his life to love. Ace was the descendant of visitors from another planet, the cosmic energy still flowing in his veins. And Peter Criss's feline features had been fostered by sabre-toothed tigers who rescued him from a plane crash. After performances, the biography declared, 'he usually finds a quiet corner to curl up in'.

All the characters were extensions of ourselves. They were characters we'd had deep inside us.
Paul Stanley, *Sounds*, 1985

In previous bands we've been in, it was each one of us who stood out – now it's a case where four people have gotten together as a cohesive and incredibly tight unit.
Gene Simmons, *Melody Maker*, 1975

35

The Kiss experience allowed their audiences to explore out their own fantasies – if you were a believer you were being given a chance to escape the humdrum of your daily routine. Critics saw their live shows as sad, unconvincing slapstick, vaudeville delivered through a 110 decibel sound system.

The stage is *A Holy Place*, you do not get up there and degrade it. If I'm paying as much to see a rock'n'roll band onstage as I would for one of their records I'm damned if I'm gonna sit there and see someone plug into a cheap little amp and have no regard for their appearance.

Gene Simmons, *NME*, 1978

We love making this kind of music. You certainly can't play intricate little ditties on the guitar and run around like a maniac, and I'll be damned if I'm going to sit on a stool!

Paul Stanley, *Sounds*, 1984

The first Kiss concert I went to I was already going out with Genie. I never really liked their music, but I was never quite impressed with a live concert as with theirs. With Gene spitting blood and Paul jumping up in the air, it was amazing. They were unbelievable.

Cher, one-time girlfriend of Gene Simmons, *Billboard*, 1989

Kiss is the greatest act since death.

Charles M. Young, *Rolling Stone*, 1977

They might not have got away with the whole act, if the band – Simmons and Stanley in particular – had not been blessed with an overweening confidence. Just as they had kicked off their stage career by disregarding the near total lack of an audience, so too they rose above the brickbats, secure in their own belief, and buoyed up by the response of their fans.

There was absolutely no doubt in any of our minds that we were just going to blow everybody off the stage.

Gene Simmons, *Billboard*, 1989

The one thing we'll never be accused of is being a Kiss copy band.

Paul Stanley, *Sounds*, 1984

When I was in the gear I felt regal, the most beautiful thing on two legs. We've never had problems with girls. And the girls know if it's memorable enough there's a song about it. All our songs are about things that happened: 'Christine Sixteen', 'Room Service', 'Fits Like A Glove'. The songs are almost sexual itineraries.

Gene Simmons, *Sounds*, 1984

NO BUSINESS LIKE SHOW BUSINESS

From day one, Messrs Simmons and Stanley had a nose (and a tongue) for business. When they hooked up with the promotional king Neil Bogart and their manager Bill Aucoin, the moneymaking motive became paramount.

Their career was always driven by commercial realities. When the stage effects began to cost tens of thousands a week, they went back in the studio just five months after the release of their not particularly successful second album 'Hotter Than Hell', to record another and generate more dollars. Realising that the excitement of the band's stage performances was their forte, they promptly released a live album. When album sales fell again in the early Eighties, they decided to create a stir by taking off the make-up. Through careful and pragmatic decisions like these, they had racked up, at the last count, in excess of 75 million album sales. And throughout their career they milked the market as much as they could, by merchandising themselves on a scale probably unsurpassed in rock'n'roll history. Like four testosterone-crazed Spice Girls, they allowed fans to identify with their favourite character nearly twenty-five years before Ginger, Scary and co. Every and any commodity that could carry a logo or a face was brought into play: pinball machines, pencil and pillow cases, tea cups and toothpaste, lunch boxes and dolls. Marvel Comics's special edition Kiss Comic Book

was that bestselling company's bestseller. There's even a rumour that there were Kiss lawnmowers – no object, it seemed, was safe. By 1978, Kiss was being cited as America's fifth largest corporation. This was not just a band, it was Kiss Inc., a conglomerate, an empire. And in the Nineties, when the band wanted to produce their own official history, they ignored the traditional publishing houses who'd turned their noses up at the million dollar advance Kiss wanted, and went ahead and published it themselves – knowing that their fans would support them. Along the way they made mistakes and errors of judgment, but more often than not their instincts were proved to be some of the shrewdest in the business.

You didn't see 'Marvel Comics presents The Eagles!'!
Paul Stanley

Perhaps the most astonishing proof of their merchandising power was the publication of Marvel's Kiss Comic Book in 1977. With typical panache, and in keeping with Gene Simmons's vampire character, Kiss agreed to donate their own blood to the ink used on the first edition – the print run was the largest in the history of Marvel, the company responsible for Spiderman, the Incredible Hulk and The Fantastic Four. None had delivered the sales muscle of Kiss, The Freaky Four.

I think Shakespeare is shit! Absolute shit! He may have been a genius for his time, but I can't relate to that stuff. 'Thee' and 'thou': he sounds like a faggot. Captain America is classic because he's more entertaining.

Gene Simmons, *Rolling Stone*, 1977

It's clear that the Kiss organisation intend to transcend the limited financial viability of rock music, just as the Kiss characters themselves become ever more unreal denizens of a fantasy world.

Paul Rambali, *NME*, 1978

We got involved in merchandising to ensure that anything that had our name on it wasn't a piece of crap.

Paul Stanley, *Melody Maker*, 1983

I didn't agree with all the merchandising – the lunch box, the cards, the dolls, etc. I didn't want us to become a teeny-bopper group, and all that merchandising was putting us in that category.

Ace Frehley

43

When former TV producer Bill Aucoin caught Kiss's act in the summer of 1973 at the Hotel Diplomat in Manhattan, much of their future act was fully fledged. What they didn't have was a deal. Aucoin liked their direction, liked their energy, and said he'd get them the deal in two weeks or they could fire him as manager. He kept his word, hooking them up with Neil Bogart of the newly formed Casablanca Records, the hustler's hustler, with plenty of money (not his, but Warner Brothers's) to burn. It was a meeting of minds.

I can honestly say that Kiss is the first band I've devoted myself 100 per cent to. In fact, they're everything I've been looking for in a rock band. Even more important is the fact that they're probably one of the best rock'n'roll bands I've ever heard in my life.

Neil Bogart, *Melody Maker*, 1975

44

NO BUSINESS LIKE SHOW BUSINESS

Bill and Neil were the real geniuses
. . . I think it was really the
management that was responsible
for making the band happen.
Ace Frehley

We wound up putting a quarter
of a million into the band before
the first year was out . . . but
there was never any real
negativity about us not making
it. The feeling was always there
that it would happen in the end.
Bill Aucoin, *Melody Maker*, 1976

Bill stepped in after we'd become
a pretty big band in New York.
We were already wearing makeup,
we had the logo and had actually
written all the songs for the first two
albums. At times he is like another
member, but in the end it's still Kiss
that runs Kiss, and we know better
than anybody what's best for us.
Paul Stanley

What Kiss Inc. demanded was total control of their career and if anybody stood in their way, the obstacle had to be removed. When Warner Brothers balked at the band's image and had second thoughts about distributing them, Casablanca took over the distribution for themselves. When Peter Criss and Ace Frehley lost the plot through drink and drugs, they were fired. And if the band members who came in to replace them didn't understand the rules, they'd soon understand that Kiss meant business.

As I rise to leave, Simmons takes me aside and says, 'Don't print anything that's gonna blow it for me. It's very fragile and I like it too much'.
Charles M. Young, *Rolling Stone*, 1977

Just recently a friend of mine recoiled in revulsion at his first exposure to Kiss, whom he termed 'everything that has left me disgusted with rock'n'roll nowadays – they're automatons!' What he failed to suss was that sometimes automatons deliver the very finest specimens of a mass-produced disposable commodity like rock.
Lester Bangs, *Creem*, 1975

Vinnie is very talented but I think he saw Kiss as a vehicle for Vinnie Vincent stardom, and unfortunately this could never be the Vinnie Vincent band.

Paul Stanley, *Sounds*, 1984

In the beginning we were tremendously jealous of the New York Dolls and we were going to do them one better. We followed their mistakes. Whatever they did wrong we never did.

Gene Simmons, *Billboard*, 1989

BEHIND THE MASK

●●●

Who were the four men behind the make-up? No one really knew. It wasn't important to the fans. What was important was that they should live out their characters to the full. And as time went on it became increasingly difficult to tell where the character and the human being crossed over. Kiss was their life. Paul Stanley was once reported as saying that if they hadn't created Kiss, they would have ended up behind bars for holding up a gas station. That might conceivably have been true of Ace Frehley and Peter Criss, both of whom had spent part of their youth in New York teenage gangs – the Hooky Boys and the Phantom Lords, respectively – but Stanley and Gene Simmons were nothing of the sort. Simmons had been trained as a teacher, and had taught for a while before he left the profession (he said he'd been teaching for the wrong reasons, plus he hated the kids). Paul Stanley was an academically trained musician. Much as they might look forward to enjoying the fame, the money and the excesses of rock stardom, they were both in dire need of a shot of street credibility, which Frehley and Criss were able to deliver. Simmons and Stanley had the vision: the other two were the essential missing ingredients. Peter Criss had been playing with a range of New York bands (one, an outfit called Chelsea, had been good enough to release an album on Decca Records) and had taken out an advert in Rolling Stone *magazine looking for work. When*

Gene Simmons had responded to the ad, his opening questions had been about Criss's appearance, not his musical experience. With the drummer in place, the search began for the final element. This time, the as yet unnamed Kiss put out their own ad, in The Village Voice. *When Ace Frehley turned up and plugged in, it all clicked.*

I'm from New York! I want it *now.* I need the ego gratification of having people tell me I'm great at the exact moment of doing what it is I'm doing, either at the moment of performing or of making a record.
Gene Simmons, *NME*, 1978

Gene Simmons was easily the most recognisable of the four, the most physically arresting: all that fire-breathing and blood-spitting, the unfeasibly large codpiece and – of course – the length of his tongue. Asked on a radio chat show once whether his tongue could reach the bridge of his nose, he came back with the one-liner 'It could reach the 59th Street Bridge!'

Girls at school would come up and say 'Stick out your tongue' and they'd giggle. Soon I became very popular and I didn't understand why. Then it dawned on me. My God, I had the power to buckle women's knees.

Gene Simmons

Bass player Gene Simmons is well to the fore. He's the guy who breathes fire in one song and a couple of minutes later starts spitting blood as he pumps out a bass-line. He also sticks his tongue out a lot and, like his comrades, poses. Of the entire band, I reckon he must feel the most stupid.

Harry Doherty, *Melody Maker*, 1976, on Kiss's UK debut

It's all right as long as he doesn't smoke or drink alcohol. I know all about his girl-friends.

Mrs Simmons, mother of Gene

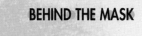

Paul Stanley had attended New York's High School of Music, and so brought the clearest musical credentials to the band. In latter years he would become the dominant songwriter, and when Gene Simmons headed off to Hollywood in the mid-Eighties to try and build-up a separate film career (it was short-lived) Stanley kept the vision and kept the band together.

We're children of the last generation of rock. All my idols, the Stones, Who, Move and the Kinks had a profound influence on my outlook on the world. When I first saw Peter of the Who, I knew that excitement could be attained and we've tried to live up to that sort of archetypal image.
Paul Stanley, *Melody Maker*, 1975

The man has presence with a capital 'P'. He flits, he flirts, he dances, he prances, his lithe body is filled with the essence of rock'n'roll.
Dave Roberts, *Sounds*, 1984

I don't believe in women trying to be me. We're two different species. You get in trouble in a relationship when they try to act like a man. Somebody needs to be in charge. I have a lot of respect for my own opinion.
Paul Stanley, *Rolling Stone*, 1977

Ace Frehley and Peter Criss were never spare parts, but they could not compete with the obsessive drive of the other two. As they drifted into drugs and booze, Simmons and Stanley unceremoniously and unsentimentally dropped the Space Ace and The Cat. Of their replacements, drummer Eric Carr – who adopted a fox character – died at 41 of cancer. Vinnie Vincent (his make-up choice was an ankh) had too much ego. And Mark St John, Bruce Kulick and Eric Singer never got to wear any make-up: they all had the regulation heavy metal hair, and were fine musicians and powerful rockers, but theirs was a time when Kiss was a different beast.

54

Peter liked to think of himself as somebody, who, like a cat, had nine lives. Somebody who grew up on the street, took chances and had gotten away with a lot.
Paul Stanley

They threw me out of the choir because I drank all the wine when I was an altar boy.
Peter Criss, *Rolling Stone*, 1977

It is my fantasy to go to another planet. By the time I'm forty, interplanetary travel will be common.
Ace Frehley, *Rolling Stone*, 1977

From the day Ace walked into an audition wearing one red sneaker and one orange one, it was obvious to the rest of us that he was very spacey. He'd talk about this mythical planet called Jendell that existed in his head.
Paul Stanley

THE KISS ARMY

In 1985, on the tenth anniversary of their first live album,
'Alive!', Kiss decided to track down the two quintessential
Seventies Kiss fans who'd been pictured on the back of the
sleeve, proudly displaying their Kiss banner in the middle of the
audience. The word went out, and the two fans were traced.
They were still fans, they still wanted to meet the band, and,
tellingly, they still had that banner. The Kiss Army was built on
such loyalty, its first regiment recruited in Terre Haute, Indiana,
when one Kiss-obsessed fan, Bill Starkey, triggered a gathering
of the forces by pestering his local radio station to play more Kiss
tracks. The band had secured up their fan base by persistent
touring; in the first years they would support any band who'd
have them – some wouldn't, notably Mott The Hoople. By playing
an incessant round of gigs, the band guaranteed long-lasting
grassroots support: it seemed that every American of a certain
age had caught Kiss fever at some point. When Kiss came to
produce a tribute album in 1995 (in typically shameless manner,
the whole venture was organised and orchestrated by their good
selves) the roster of artists who wanted to be involved went way
beyond the obvious heavy metal copyists, spanning Garth Brooks
and Stevie Wonder, the Lemonheads and Lenny Kravitz – and
the grunge acts out of Seattle were happy to acknowledge their

debt. The fan base was international. Kiss had cracked Japan early on, with a sell-out record matched only by The Beatles and Michael Jackson. The UK, a slow starter, had built-up to become one of the band's most supportive markets. In each territory Kiss conventions kept the flame of Kissmania alive, and by the time the original line-up reunited in 1996, that flame was burning as fiercely as ever. When they announced the first date of the reunion tour, at Tiger Stadium in Detroit (the band's home from home), the gig sold out in 47 minutes, a venue record.

Growing up in the suburbs, a few of my friends and I were heavily into Kiss. They never really got their songs played on the radio or anything, so it was almost as if they were an underground band, even though they obviously sold plenty of records.

Thurston Moore, Sonic Youth

The fans believed in the band. The band believed in the fans. It was the perfect relationship. (The cynics, meantime, contented themselves with sneering that Kiss only truly believed in the bottomless pockets of their fans.)

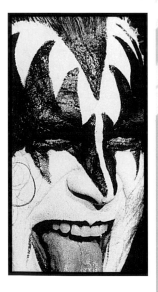

It wasn't too long ago when we were in the audience and paying. The whole premise of Kiss was that when you're paying to see us, we feel we owe you everything.

Paul Stanley, *Melody Maker*, 1975

When you talk about a band like Kiss you're talking about playing venues that hold 50 – 150,000 people. To have the charisma to become that popular you must be a Zeppelin or a Stones or a Deep Purple. Any Mid-West garage band has twice the charisma of The Clash. Before people go and see The Clash they should see the new US bands like . . . like Van Halen. Now *they* kill . . . .

Gene Simmons, *NME*, 1978

When we were putting Chic together, we decided that the ultimate disco band would be a group that incorporated the style of Roxy Music and the power, energy and theatrics of Kiss.

Nile Rodgers, *Billboard*, 1989

My biggest influence through junior high was Kiss. That was my thing.

Garth Brooks

I started playing guitar because of Kiss. To me, they were the biggest band in the world.

Mike McCready, Pearl Jam

NO BEAST SO FIERCE

Alongside the adolescent footsoldiers, guys who could only wet-dream of being as all-conquering as their Kiss heroes, there came a stream of camp-followers who were happy to fulfil the band's own fantasies. Gene Simmons may have abstained from alcohol and drugs, but he and Stanley were happy to feast on the sexual favours granted by their female fans, and ever ready to boast about their apparently insatiable appetites: they had experienced everything, claimed Simmons, 'up to but excluding farm animals'.

The womanising stuff always pops up. The womanising stuff . . . *exists*, but if you believe half of what you read then we've bedded down every woman and her daughter in the world. Close to the truth but not totally.

Gene Simmons, *Melody Maker*, 1988

His love and passion flow from every pore, touching people of all ages and both sexes. This extraordinary gift is transmitted through his music, creating an atmosphere of love that permeates every core of his universe.

Paul Stanley's publicity 'biography'

It's the reason I first put a guitar around my neck. I wanna get laid after the show. If I was playing Celtic mountain music maybe I'd have different conversations, but I'd still want to get fucked. It's all sex.

Gene Simmons, *Sounds*, 1988

The Army was invincible during the mid-Seventies. Kiss had been taken to the hearts of their fans, and even the older generations, who should have been appalled, seemed to be entranced. There seemed to be endless photo opportunities with local fire crews, police chiefs and little old ladies on London buses. It was the music critics and the musicians who could not bestow praise. If these jokers, who had no aesthetic aims or claims, could be hugely successful, it undermined the whole point of taking rock'n'roll so seriously . . . .

When Kiss hit town they get the works: keys, red carpets and police escorts. Kind of fishy for a bunch of perverted looking dudes in monster make-up and ten-inch heels, the kind of guys you'd expect your parents to loathe and detest. But no, the Kiss armies, kissing competitions, Kiss-mobiles and fan clubs abound, the accent is on fun-a-go-go.

Max Bell, *NME, 1976*

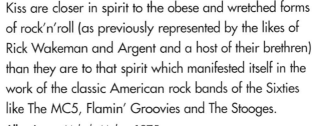

Kiss are closer in spirit to the obese and wretched forms of rock'n'roll (as previously represented by the likes of Rick Wakeman and Argent and a host of their brethren) than they are to that spirit which manifested itself in the work of the classic American rock bands of the Sixties like The MC5, Flamin' Groovies and The Stooges.

Allan Jones, *Melody Maker*, 1975

I suppose even after eating a can of beans, every little fart is its own self-contained composition – but perhaps I'm being too kind. Kiss is an essay on rock mannerisms, and stale ones at that.

Chrissie Hynde, 1974, on the album 'Kiss'

Rock'n'roll is not meant to be criticized. If you can find someone who's willing to pay you to be a critic, then you've found a sucker.

Paul Stanley

MUSICAL MOMENTS

●●

Behind the escapism, the horny lyrics, the costumes and the make-up, the theatricality of it all, it's easy to forget there was actually some music. Nothing of any great originality, maybe, but a driving heavy metal sound nonetheless. Gene Simmons has said that when they set out to form Kiss, they wanted to play the music that excited them. Their roots were out of the loud British bands who'd made an impact on American audiences – The Stones and The Who, Humble Pie, Led Zeppelin. Ace Frehley's role models for lead guitar were Jimmy Page and Jeff Beck. Mix that up with a dash of Arthur Brown, Alice Cooper and Slade, and you had the Kiss sound. Only Peter Criss claimed a different starting point: he was a Phil Spector man, a fan of the Ronettes, Marvin Gaye and the Four Tops. As the band's career lengthened, the albums matured a little, but not much. The main thrust of any critique was how well each album had been able to capture the thunder of their live performances. Whenever they moved away from the formula, they had mixed fortunes. On 'Destroyer', their fifth album, they broadened their range with additional musicians, and the album still sold (although this was 1976, with Kissmania rampant, and their fans would probably have bought anything they released). But 1981's '(Music From) The Elder', a concept album based around a mystical short story by Gene Simmons, and released when concept albums were already

prehistoric, failed completely by Kiss's exacting commercial standards. They realised their mistake, and on the next album, 'Creatures Of The Night', promptly went back to basics. Safe, simple and successful.

Rock and roll is for the true believers who really understand what's going on and not people who want it diluted. I think pure rock and roll, good rock and roll, has the same thing that anything that's pure has – and that's honesty. Unthinking, primal honesty.

Paul Stanley, *Sounds*, 1984

'Dressed To Kill' was the band's third album; the first two had failed to find much chart success, and with no hit single radio play was thin on the ground. Written at speed, produced by the band and Neil Bogart, the spontaneous energy of the album took Kiss into the US Top 40 for the first time, putting them on the verge of major record sales. A hit single remained elusive, but the sessions produced the durable Kiss anthem 'Rock And Roll All Nite'.

The first thing to hit you about this album is the sheer cunning of the sleeve design. The deliberate drabness of the black and white picture with the black background are a brilliant contrast to the title. It's one for the album sleeve connoisseur.

Esdale Maclean, *Melody Maker*, 1975

Neil said to us, 'You guys need an anthem'. At that time, rock bands didn't have anthems, but Neil was smart and really ahead of his time. He said Sly and the Family Stone had 'I Want To Take You Higher'. So we came up with 'Rock And Roll All Nite'.

Paul Stanley

I conclude that this is one of the most expendable, vapid formulations of the time-tested excursions into nowhere since Lord Rutherford tried to stick the atom back together again. And being one of the only people in this office who liked their two previous albums it comes as some disappointment to be presented with such tired mill-grist by way of the third.

Max Bell, *NME*, 1975

Disappointed by the sales of the first three albums, and determined to reflect the in-concert enthusiasm of their fans, Kiss, unlike bands who fall back on live recordings to pad out their release schedule, decided to use the live album as a central plank of their strategy. It paid off, handsomely. 'Alive!', a double disk of the best of their material, recorded principally at Cobo Hall, Detroit, went straight to Number 9 in the US charts, and 'Rock And Roll All Nite', re-released as a single, reached Number 12.

'Alive!' broke at the right time, because we were broke and so were the record label, Casablanca. Our record sales were pretty soft, but we were building this huge reputation as a live band. We figured that either people didn't like the records or else they didn't capture what we were like live. We felt that we needed to give people a souvenir of the live show.

Paul Stanley

They lack the essential concentration and stunning precision which was the hallmark of The MC5 at their glorious best, or the manic force of The Stooges. There's not even that sense of transitory cheap thrills one got from listening to the first New York Dolls' album.

Allan Jones, *Melody Maker*, 1975

It captures for us exactly what we were. It captured the live insanity, the adrenalin, it captured the audience's vibes with our vibes.

Peter Criss

'Destroyer' was Kiss's first attempt, in Paul Stanley's words – to write something beyond 'suck me, fuck me' songs. It also marked the arrival of Bob Ezrin, Alice Cooper's producer, and the addition of an orchestra and session guitarists (much to Ace Frehley's annoyance). Frequently voted by Kiss fans as their favourite album, it was the first to go platinum, the first to chart in the UK, and produced the Top Ten single 'Beth', a ballad written and sung by drummer Peter Criss.

For 'Destroyer' they've kept the services of Bob Ezrin, who is certainly a better producer than Neil Bogart, and heralds Kiss' foray into the territory vacated by Alice Cooper now that he's taken to advertising Budweiser and playing golf with the establishment.

Max Bell, *NME*, 1976

The key to building a superstar is keeping their mouths shut. They have to be kept isolated to avoid being manipulated by all these outside forces. There was a time when Kiss weren't allowed to talk to anyone.

'Destroyer' producer **Bob Ezrin**, *Rolling Stone*, 1977

Kiss retread old territory that has been covered so well over the years that their contribution to rock is negligible; and, although they do well by all the clichés, their future, at the level of staidness displayed on 'Destroyer' can only be brief.

Harry Doherty, *Melody Maker*, 1976

Opening night of the new tour was in Detroit, a city so close to Kiss's heart that they'd written 'Detroit Rock City' in celebration of the intensity of its inhabitants' passion for the band. And so it went on, in Cleveland, in New York's Madison Square Garden, headlining the annual Donnington metal festival in the UK. Like the tyrannosaurus rex in Jurassic Park, Kiss were back with a bite.

Everything you've heard about the Kiss years and the Kiss shows and the Kiss spectacle is true. It's not legend. We're going to show every new band how the big boys do it. We're going to get up on that stage and collectively Kiss your ass.

Gene Simmons, 1996

Once we did Unplugged, which was the first time the four of us had played together in sixteen years, I think we all sensed that the chemistry was still there.

Ace Frehley, 1996

The other three guys have to be with me . . . they are my other powers. I couldn't be as strong without the others around . . . . I never felt happier in my life.

Peter Criss, 1996

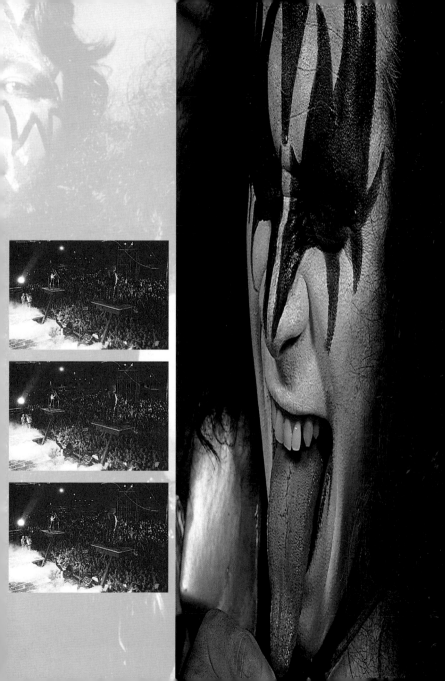

Although their bravado was as youthful as ever, and the durability of the Kiss formula undimmed, the band had to go into a programme of physical training in addition to the usual rehearsals. After all, striding around a stage wearing eight-inch platform boots in your late forties saps the strength from the ageing muscles of even the most self-confident superhero.

The best diet for the road is soup for lunch and candy for supper. It keeps the weight off and you're speeding on all that sugar by show time.
Paul Stanley, *Rolling Stone*, 1977

Any band which bases its appeal on the admiration of the turbulent hormones of pre-teens is bound to suffer from built-in obsolence just like those gross Detroit vehicles with the absurd pink fins on the ass end . . . . Possibly the worst album of all time!
Sandy Robertson, *Sounds*, 1985, review of 'Asylum'

We've never been a band based on fads. We've always done things our way. Probably the reason we've lasted this long is that what we do is timeless.
Paul Stanley, *Billboard*, 1989

By the time of the reunion there was speculation that the band would perform through to 1999, and then split up. If and when they decided to call it a day, Kiss would live behind one central question: was their career sheer genius, or the biggest rock'n'roll swindle of all?

Before HM, Kiss was heavy rock. Before heavy rock, Kiss was rock'n'roll . . . and so on.

Paul Stanley, *Sounds*, 1985

Like H. P. Barnum said, you can fool some of the people all of the time . . . but who would have thought that all you need to do it is overgrown platform boots and stick-on Hallowe'en masks?

Paul Rambali, *NME*, 1978

I don't want to sound malicious, but with people like the New York Dolls . . . well, you can't go on fooling audiences all the time. We can play. Before this came together we were practising for months in a loft to get it right.

Gene Simmons, *NME*, 1975

Kiss is a life-style, it's a force, it's a pack of dogs – it's whatever you want it to be.

Paul Stanley

THE MUSIC

★★★★★   **Essential listening**

★★★   **OK**

★   **Frankly, not the best!**

SINGLES
Rock'n'Roll All Nite/Getaway – May 1975 ★★★★★
Beth/Detroit Rock City – August 1976 ★★★★¹/₂
Hard Luck Woman/Mr. Speed – December 1976 ★★★★
Calling Dr. Love/Take Me – June 1977 ★★★
Christine Sixteen/Shock Me – July 1977 ★★¹/₂
Rocket Ride/Tomorrow And Tonight (Live) –
   February 1978 ★★¹/₂
I Was Made For Lovin' You/Hard Times – June 1979 ★★★★
Crazy Crazy Nights/No, No, No – October 1987 ★★★★
Forever/The Street Giveth And The Street Taketh Away – March 1990 ★★★
God Gave Rock'n'Roll To You II/Junior's Gone Wild – January 1992 ★★★★

ALBUMS
Kiss – February 1974 ★★★
Strutter/Nothin' To Lose/Firehouse/Cold Gin/Let Me Know/Kissin' Time/Deuce/Love Theme From Kiss/100,000 Years/Black Diamond
A first album of unbelievable ferocity. Try 'Strutter' which is not the high camp posturing you'd imagine – no scout masters in this set-up. Under all that make-up they leer like four Joel Grays.
Max Bell, *NME, 1975*

Hotter Than Hell – November 1974 ★★★
Got To Choose/Parasite/Goin' Blind/Hotter Than Hell/Let Me Go/ Rock'n'Roll All The Way/Watchin' You/Mainline/Comin' Home/Strange Ways
The band underwent exhaustive touring to promote 'Hotter Than Hell', along with 'Kiss' and 'Dressed To Kill'. Many of these early gigs were the catalyst which engendered fervent members of the later-to-emerge Kiss Army.

Dressed To Kill – March 1975 ★★★
Room Service/Two Timer/Ladies In Waiting/Getaway/Rock Bottom/C'mon And
Love Me/Anything For My Baby/She/Love Her All I Can/Rock And Roll All Nite
*The heavy crashing chord formula is kept up relentlessly apart from on the
opening to 'Rock Bottom' which is a simple line played and interplayed over again
on acoustic guitars. Simple, but effective.*
Esdale Maclean, *Melody Maker, 1975*

Alive! – September 1975 ★★★★¹/₂
Deuce/Strutter/Got To Choose/Hotter Than Hell/Firehouse/Nothin' To Lose/C'mon
And Love Me/Parasite/She/Watchin' You/100,000 Years/Black Diamond/Rock
Bottom/Cold Gin/Rock And Roll All Nite/Let Me Go/Rock'n'Roll
*This was Kiss's breakthrough album, finally gaining them a place in the US Top 10,
and becoming their first certified US platinum album. A rock god of vinyl.*

Destroyer – May 1976 ★★★
Detroit Rock City/King Of The Night Time World/God Of Thunder/Great
Expectations/Flaming Youth/Sweet Pain/Shout It Out Loud/Beth/Do You Love Me
There's no doubt that 'Destroyer' is Kiss's best album yet.
John Milward, *Rolling Stone,* 3 June, 1976

Rock And Roll Over – November 1976 ★★¹/₂
I Want You/Take Me/Calling Dr. Love/Ladies Room/Baby Driver/Love 'Em And
Leave 'Em/Mr. Speed/See You In Your Dreams/Hard Luck Woman/Makin' Love

Love Gun June 1977 ★★★
I Stole Your Love/Christine Sixteen/Got Love For Sale/Shock Me/Tomorrow And
Tonight/Love Gun/Hooligan/Almost Human/Plaster Caster/Then She Kissed Me
*The band's bestselling album so far, 'Love Gun' stormed the US charts ending up at
Number 4. Possibly the most memorable and well-known of all their album cover designs.*

Kiss Alive II – October 1977 ★★★★
Detroit Rock City/King Of The Night Time World/Ladies Room/Makin' Love/Love
Gun/Calling Dr. Love/Christine Sixteen/Shock Me/Hard Luck Woman/Tomorrow And
Tonight/I Stole Your Love/Beth/God Of Thunder/I Want You/Shout It Loud/All American
Man/Rockin' In The USA/Larger Than Life/Rocket Ride/Any Way You Want It
Really the greatest live album of this year. Conceivably of the decade. Possibly of the century.
Geoff Barton, *Sounds, 1977*

Dynasty – June 1979 ★★★¹/₂
I Was Made For Lovin' You/2,000 Man/Sure Know Something/Dirty
Livin'/Charisma/Magic Touch/Hard Times/X-Ray Eyes/Save Your Love
'Kiss-do disco' not only rhymes sweetly but surprisingly describes the first track on

their new album . . . Called 'I Was Made For Lovin' You', it is rich in Moroderisms and looks destined to be a chart hit.
Steve Gett, *Melody Maker, 1979*

Unmasked – June 1980 ★★★
Is That You?/Shandi/Talk To Me/Naked City/What Makes The World Go Round/Tomorrow/Two Sides Of The Coin/She's So European/Easy As It Seems/Torpedo Girl/You're All That I Want
Musically, there are few surprises . . . 'Unmasked' may not mark any 'progression', but it's enjoyable, nonetheless.
Steve Gett, *Melody Maker, 1980*

(Music From) The Elder – November 1981 ★★
The Oath/Fanfare/Just A Boy/Dark Light/Only You/Under The Rose/A World Without Heroes/Mr. Blackwell/Escape From The Island/ Odyssey I

Lick It Up – September 1983 ★★★
Exciter/Not For The Innocent/Lick It Up/Young And Waster/Gimme More/All Hell's Breakin' Loose/A Million To One/Fits Like A Glove/Dance All Over Your Face/And On The 8th Day
'Lick It Up' went to Number 24 in the US charts and Number 7 in the UK – giving the band their first UK Top 10 placing. It was the first album after their official 'unmasking' on MTV and, as such, marked a new phase in the Kiss career.

Animalize – September 1984 ★★½
I've Had Enough (Into The Fire)/Heaven's On Fire/Burn Bitch Burn/Get All You Can Take/Lonely Is The Hunter/Under The Gun/Thrills In The Night/While The City Sleeps/Murder In High-Heels

Asylum – September 1985 ★★★
King Of The Mountain/Any Way You Slice It/Who Wants To Be Lonely/Trial By Fire/I'm Alive/Love's A Deadly Weapon/Tears Are Falling/Secretly Cruel/Radar For Love/Uh! All Night
'Asylum' made the US Top 20 and UK Number 12, though the single 'Tears Are Falling' was not as well received. It reached only Number 51 in the US and Number 57 in the UK.

Crazy Nights – September 1987 ★★★
Crazy Crazy Nights/I'll Fight Hell To Hold You/Bang Bang You/No, No, No/Hell On High Water/My Way/When Your Walls Come Down/Reason To Live/Good Girl Gone Bad/Turn On The Night/Thief In The Night
The album which featured the band's biggest ever UK single, the eponymous 'Crazy, Crazy Nights'. It charted at Number 4, proving the allegiance of the UK Kiss Army.

Smashes, Thrashes And Hits – November 1988 ★★★★¹/₂
Let's Put The X In Sex/Crazy Crazy Nights/(You Make Me) Rock Hard/Love Gun/Detroit Rock City/I Love It Loud/Reason To Live/Lick It Up/ Heaven's On Fire/Calling Dr. Love/Strutter /Beth/Tears Are Falling/I Was Made For Lovin' You/Rock And Roll All Nite/Shout It Out Loud
This career-spanning grab bag . . . [is]. . . the most consistently listenable Kiss album by far.
Mark Coleman, *Rolling Stone Album Guide,* 1992

Revenge – May 1992 ★★★
Unholy/Take It Off/Tough Love/Spit/God Gave Rock'n'Roll To You II/Domino/Heart Of Chrome/Thou Shalt Not/Every Time I Look At You/Paralyzed/I Just Wanna/Carr Jam 1981
Kiss are a band well capable of softening their hard rock to chart-acceptable consistency: witness the recent success of 'God Gave Rock And Roll To You II'. Though the track is on 'Revenge', much of the rest of the album is spikier and weightier than accepted Kiss style.
Jeff Clark-Meads, *Q magazine,* 1992

Kiss Alive III – May 1993 ★★★
Creatures Of The Night/Deuce/I Just Wanna/Unholy/Heaven's On Fire/Watchin' You/Domino/I Was Made For Lovin' You/I Still Love You/Rock and Roll All Nite/Lick It Up/Take It Off/I Love It Loud/Detroit Rock City/God Gave Rock'n'Roll To You II/Star Spangled Banner
'Alive III' (along with 'Revenge') featured Eric Singer on drums. Many fans felt the band had reclaimed their early Seventies roots on this album, with their celebrated renditions of such classics as 'Creatures Of The Night' and 'Unholy'.

THE HISTORY

Key Dates

January 1973
Kiss is formed by ex-Wicked Lesters Paul Stanley and Gene Simmons when that band breaks up. They recruit Peter Criss from a *Rolling Stone* ad he's inserted, and Ace Frehley via an ad they've placed in *Village Voice*. First gig as Kiss is a three-night residency at a club in Queens – Peter Criss later recalls that the entire audience consists of Gene Simmons's girlfriend and two other friends. Although the promo pack the band have prepared shows them barefaced, they perform from the start with full make-up.

July 1973
After recording demos with Eddie Kramer at the Electric Ladyland studios, the band's turning point is a showcase at the Hotel Diplomat in Manhattan which generates a good review in *Variety*, the entertainment industry's newspaper. Bill Aucoin, a former TV show producer, sees them there the following month, offers to manage them and engineers a deal with Neil Bogart of Casablanca Records. They are the label's first major signing.

December 1973
Kiss appear with Blue Oyster Cult, Iggy Pop & The Stooges and Teenage Lust at a New Year's Eve event at the New York Academy of Music.

January 1974
Kiss are the last act to perform at Bill Graham's Fillmore East.

February 1974
The debut album 'Kiss', its sleeve a spoof of 'Meet The Beatles' shot by the Doors's photographer Joel Brodsky, is launched by Casablanca with lashings of hype. The album hits the US Top 100 and stays in the charts for 23 weeks, eventually going gold.

April 1975
After a disappointing second album, Kiss's third, 'Dressed To Kill', co-produced by Casablanca boss Neil Bogart and the band, becomes their first Top 40 album. In the meantime, the band has been assiduously building up its fan base though rigorous, extensive touring, opening as the support for acts as unlikely as Rory Gallagher, Savoy Brown and Manfred Mann (although Mott The Hoople refuse to let them tour).

November 1975
The live album 'Alive!', recorded at a string of dates and capturing the power and pizazz of the live show, cracks the US Top 10. 'Rock And Roll All Nite', the single off the album, is a chart success. Kiss's legions of fans get a formal identity as the Kiss Army, which is founded in Indiana where a dedicated fan, one Bill Starkey, pesters his local radio station to play Kiss tracks, sparking an outpouring of support. Kissmania is born.

February 1976
Only two years after the debut album, Kiss are already successful enough to be asked to immortalise their footprints outside Grauman's Chinese Theater in Hollywood. The band now do not appear in public unless they are in full make-up.

April 1976
'Destroyer' – produced by Bob Ezrin, Alice Cooper's collaborator on albums like 'School's Out' – is Kiss's first platinum success (peaking at Number 11 in the US charts and later Number 22 in the UK, the band's first chart success there). New costumes are designed for the band by Jules Fisher Associates.

May 1976
Kiss play their first ever UK date at Manchester's Free Trade Hall, and then play London's Hammersmith Odeon, with a significantly reduced stage show.

July 1976
Casablanca re-release the first three studio albums as a boxed set called 'The Originals', containing an additional 16-page booklet, photo cards and stickers. A 'limited edition' of 250,000 units are pressed. The run is virtually an instant sell-out.

MoDERN iCoNS — KISS

November 1976
First official gathering of the Kiss Army. 21
November is declared Kiss Day. Gene Simmons's
tongue is banned on American TV, cameras cut
away every time he opens his mouth in close-up.
He is banned from spitting blood on TV.

December 1976
The ballad 'Beth' sung and written by drummer Pete Criss reaches Number 7 in
the States, but garners little interest in the UK. A 15-year-old fan who tries to copy
Simmons's fire-spitting act – after seeing it on TV – burns 35% of his upper body.
The band reissue warnings to fans not to try and imitate their stage act. Ace
Frehley receives an electric shock during a show at Lakeland, Florida, but survives
unscathed. Minutes later Gene Simmons sets himself alight.

March 1977
Tickets go on sale for a Kiss concert in Detroit's 12,000-seat Cobo Hall. In Duluth,
a youth demands three tickets at gunpoint. The same month, Kiss have huge
success in Japan.

April 1977
'Beth' ties with 'Disco Duck' for Best Song of the Year in the People's Choice
awards.

June 1977
Marvel Comics launch a Kiss feature series with *The Kiss Comic Book*, written by
Steve Gerber who also produces *Howard the Duck*. Each member of group
donates some blood towards the ink mix! The comic sells 400,000 copies, a
Marvel record until the Eighties.

September 1977
'Love Gun' gets to the US Number 4 slot, having been certified platinum on
advance orders. It is Kiss's best-selling album to date.

October 1977
Gene Simmons loses two inches of his hair and scorches the right side of his neck,
when his fire-breathing section of the show goes wrong during a performance in
Los Angeles.

November 1977
'Kiss Alive II' recorded in August during three shows at the Great Western Forum, Inglewood, California gets to US Number 7, bringing the band their fourth platinum disc. The fourth side of studio recordings includes session guitar work by Rick Derringer and Bob Kulick – Ace has gone AWOL.

October 1978
Simultaneously the four band members release their debut solo albums. Sales are disappointing although in true Casablanca records style 1.25 million of each are shipped (it was said of Casablanca that 'they shipped gold but returned platinum'). Critics consider Paul Stanley has stayed closest to the Kiss sound, but the highest placed of the four is Gene Simmons's effort, reaching US Number 22. However, the highest chart position is secured by an Ace Frehley single 'New York Groove'. NBC premieres the band's animated movie *Kiss Meets The Phantom Of The Park.*

June 1979
The band's next album, 'Dynasty' is a return to form after the solo ventures, another Top 10 hit. Significantly Pete Criss plays on only a handful of the tracks, having been involved in a serious auto accident while under the influence of various substances. Session man Anton Fig fills in on the remaining tracks.

May 1980
Criss leaves Kiss. The usual line about 'musical differences' is trotted out: the reality is that the band fire him because of his drink and drugs problems. He is replaced by Eric Carr.

December 1981
'(Music From) The Elder', a concept album based around a Gene Simmons's short story, performs disappointingly. Lou Reed is involved in the lyric writing.

November 1982
The album 'Creatures Of The Night' is dedicated to Casablanca Records's Neil Bogart who has recently died of cancer. Ace Frehley's contribution to the album is unclear. In a bizarre echo of the Peter Criss episode, Ace Frehley is injured in a car crash. His work is covered by Vinnie Vincent, Robben Ford and Steven Ferris. Ace then leaves the band, to deal with addiction problems. Vinnie Vincent is installed to replace Frehley.

June 1983
In Sao Paulo, Brazil, Kiss give their last concert in
full make-up before they unmask.

September 1983
Kiss are finally unmasked, by choice, on MTV, after
eighteen albums in make-up, and appear likewise
on their next album release, 'Lick It Up', their first album for Mercury Records.

January 1984
Mark St John replaces Vinnie Vincent – who has been fired after proving unable to
fit into the Kiss operation – but his involvement is cut short through illness: he is
diagnosed as having the rare Reiter's syndrome. St John is in turn replaced by Bob
Kulick the following year.

October 1984
Kiss get back to platinum sales with 'Animalize' (Number 19 in the States, Number
11 in the UK).

December 1985
Kiss's show at Madison Square Gardens, NYC, earns the band fifth place in that
year's top ten list of concert grosses. Simmons appears in the film *Runaway*.

November 1987
'Crazy Crazy Nights' is their most successful UK single, as is the similarly titled
album, both reaching Number 4.

August 1988
Kiss play the Monsters of Rock festival at Castle Donnington, supporting headliners
Guns 'N Roses. Gene Simmons launches his own record label, Simmons.

April 1990
'Forever', written by Paul Stanley and Michael Bolton, is their first US Top 10
single since 'Beth' in 1976.

February 1991
On Phil Donahue's talk show, former drummer Peter Criss appears to dispel
bizarre claims from a man who asserts he is Peter Criss in a US tabloid.

November 1991
Kiss drummer Eric Carr dies in a New York hospital following a cerebral haemorrhage which has complicated the cancer he is already suffering from. The band's album 'Revenge' and Slaughter's album 'Wild Life' are dedicated to him.

April 1992
With Carr's replacement, Eric Singer, in place, a muted tour begins.

May 1992
'Revenge' produced by Bob Ezrin – who previously produced 'Destroyer' for Kiss – reaches Number 6 in the States and Number 10 in the UK.

July 1994
The tribute album 'Kiss My Ass' is released. Tears For Fears, Ozzy Osbourne and the Stone Temple Pilots are some of the acts who want to take part but are prevented by legal reasons. The successful line-ups include Lenny Kravitz and Stevie Wonder (performing 'Deuce'), Garth Brooks ('Hard Luck Woman'), the Lemonheads ('Plaster Caster') and Extreme ('Strutter').

May 1995
The band self-publish *Kisstory*, their own story in a $160, 9lb volume.

August 1995
An MTV Unplugged session includes appearances by both Peter Criss and Ace Frehley, alongside current members Eric Singer and Bruce Kulick, fuelling speculation that the original Kiss is about to reform.

April 1996
Following a surprise appearance at the 1996 Grammy Awards ceremony, the anticipated reunion is announced at a press conference aboard the American Navy aircraft carrier USS Intrepid. Eric Singer and Bruce Kulick take a paid sabbatical while the Simmons, Stanley, Criss and Frehley line-up undertake a major tour, opening in Detroit in June, and including a headlining appearance at the UK's Donnington heavy metal festival.

THE CAST

Bill Aucoin. Kiss's first manager sees the band at one of their showcase gigs at New York's Hotel Diplomat. He and his business partner Joyce Biawitz, have been the producers of a TV music show in the early Seventies, through which connection they know Neil Bogart (Joyce Biawitz later becomes the second Mrs Neil Bogart).

Neil Bogart. Born Neil Bogatz, 1943, Brooklyn, NY. The head of Casablanca Records is a legend within the record business. After attending the New York School of Performing Arts (of *Fame* fame) he releases a few recordings as a vocalist – the single 'Bobby' reaching Number 58 in the US charts in 1962 – before moving into the promotion side of the music industry where his real talents flourish. After a stint as the general manager of Buddha Records, home of artificially created bubblegum acts like Ohio Express and 1910 Fruitgum Company, he gets backing from Warner to found Casablanca Records in 1973 (Bogart – Casablanca, geddit?). Casablanca quickly gains a reputation for huge promotions and a drug-fuelled Californian lifestyle. Kiss is Casablanca's first big act and is a much needed cash cow for the record company, who go on to sign Donna Summer, Cher (Simmons's sometime girlfriend), Parliament and the Village People. Casablanca is sold by Bogart to PolyGram in the late Seventies – the financial black hole they inherit causes them problems for years to come. Bogart, who has also worked with acts ranging from the Isleys to Melanie and whose over the top vision is a critical part of the Kiss phenomenon, dies of cancer in May 1982. Kiss dedicate their next album, 'Creatures Of The Night', to Bogart's memory.

Eric Carr. Born 12 July 1950, Brooklyn, NY. Is in a covers band during the Seventies before the Kiss audition – to replace Peter Criss in 1980 – comes along. Carr is a central part of Kiss throughout the Eighties, but in 1991 has to undergo open heart surgery. Cancer is discovered. In September that year he suffers a cerebral haemorrhage and dies on 24 November, on the same day as Freddie Mercury.

Peter Criss. Born Peter Crisscoula, 27 December 1945, Brooklyn, NY. Is in various bands before Simmons and Stanley spot his ad in *Rolling Stone*, including Barracuda, Chelsea (who release an album on Decca), and an outfit called Lips. While with Lips he writes the ballad 'Beth' which – with his vocals – is a smash hit for Kiss in 1976, followed up by another Criss-written and sung single 'Hard Luck Woman'. After being fired from Kiss in May 1980 he pursues a solo career, releasing the albums 'Out Of Control' and 'Let Me Rock You', before joining the band Balls Of Fire. Marries Playboy centrefold Debra Svensk. He later releases another solo album, 'Criss', in 1993, before getting back together with his former colleagues in 1995.

Ace Frehley. Born Paul Frehley, 22 April 1951, Bronx, NY. Is reportedly the 61st guitarist auditioned by Simmons and Stanley: has previously played in a number of power rock outfits. He completes the original line-up. Sees solo success while with Kiss when 'New York Groove', released as part of the four Kiss members's solo activities in 1978, gets to Number 13 in the US. After a serious car crash in 1982, he leaves the band, and then spends four years dealing with his drug addiction. Between 1987-89 he returns to the music business with a new band, Frehley's Comet, releasing four albums: the highest-placed is their 1987 debut 'Frehley's Comet', which reaches US Number 43. Reconvenes with Simmons and Stanley in 1995.

Bruce Kulick. After missing the guitar spot in Kiss first time round – despite contributing to the studio side of 'Alive II' in Frehley's frequent absences – when Vinnie Vincent steps in for Frehley, Kulick eventually lands the job when Vincent's replacement Mark St John is forced to retire through illness. Like Eric Singer, when the original Kiss reunite in 1995-96, he takes a long break, running a series of musicians' clinics.

Mark St John. Born Mark Norton. He replaces Vinnie Vincent who has been fired by the rest of the band in January 1994. Sadly for St John he is unable to establish a regular presence in the band, as it is discovered that he is suffering from Reiter's syndrome. He has to relinquish the guitar spot only a year after joining, and his place is taken by Bruce Kulick.

MoDERN iCoNS — KISS

Gene Simmons. Born Chaim Witz, 25 August 1949, Haifa, Israel. He arrives in New York at age nine, eventually training and working as a teacher while playing in various garage bands until he decides to abandon the teaching profession entirely, forming first a trio called Rainbow, and then Wicked Lester with Paul Stanley in 1971-72. Wicked Lester get as far as recording an album for Epic (never released), although the cover artwork mysteriously turns up on a 1979 CBS release by Laughing Dogs. Simmons and Stanley then set about creating the Kiss phenomenon and remain the driving force and controlling influences at its heart from then on. In the Eighties, Simmons flirts with movie stardom, starring with Tom Selleck in the Michael Crichton-written and directed *Runaway* (1984), as well as taking parts in 1986's *Never Too Young To Die* and *Trick Or Treat*, and making a cameo appearance in *Miami Vice*. Having produced Wendy O. Williams, Japanese metal act E-Z-O and Black N Blue, he launches his record label, Simmons, in 1988: the first signings are US acts The Hunger and The House Of Lords.

Eric Singer. Born Cleveland, Ohio. Drums for a short while with Black Sabbath in 1986, as well as the band Badlands and joins Kiss in 1992 following Eric Carr's death in 1991. When the original Kiss reforms, Singer, like Bruce Kulick, takes an open-ended, paid sabbatical.

Paul Stanley. Born Paul Stanley Eisen, 20 January 1950, Queens, NY. Stanley, a graduate of the New York High School of Music, meets Gene Simmons briefly when Simmons plays with Stanley's band Uncle Joe. He later auditions for Simmons's band, the trio Rainbow, in 1971 and is invited to join. The band later becomes Wicked Lester, before Stanley and Simmons decide to evolve into Kiss. Stanley develops his songwriting skills, has songs recorded by Bonnie Tyler, and co-writes 'I Was Made For Loving You' with Desmond Child. He tours solo in 1989 with a band containing Bob Kulick and (then not yet a Kiss member) Eric Singer.

Vinnie Vincent. Born Vincent Cusano. Joins Kiss in 1982, taking over as guitarist after Ace Frehley's departure. He never really fits in and is fired for 'unethical behaviour' in 1984. After Kiss, he forms the Vinnie Vincent Invasion: neither their 1986 debut album 'Vinnie Vincent Invasion' or the follow-up 'All Systems Go' trouble the US Top 50. Gene Simmons later memorably remarks: 'Vinnie was in the band for a short time, and then he was let go. He was also let go from a band called the Vinnie Vincent Invasion, which is a tough thing to do! That might give you a clue about what's wrong with Vinnie.'

THE BOOKS

Kiss: Revenge Is Sweet – Joe Stevens (Omnibus) 1997
Kiss: The Hottest Band In The World – Michael Heatley (UFO) 1997

PICTURE CREDITS

Pages 2-3 Fin Costello/Redferns. **Page 5** Fin Costello/Redferns. **Page 8** Frank Forcino/London Features International (LFI). **Page 11** Kevin Mazur/LFI. **Page 12** LFI. **Page 13** Kevin Mazur/LFI. **Page 14** Richie Aaron/Redferns. **Page 15** Fin Costello/Redferns. **Page 16** Fin Costello/Redferns. **Page 17** Paul Bergen/Redferns. **Page 19** Fin Costello/Redferns. **Page 20** Fin Costello/Redferns. **Page 21** Fin Costello/Redferns. **Page 22** Mick Hutson/Redferns. **Page 23** Fin Costello/Redferns. **Page 25** (t) Fin Costello/Redferns; (b) Fin Costello/Redferns. **Page 26** Fin Costello/Redferns. **Page 27** Fin Costello/Redferns. **Page 29** LFI. **Page 31** Ebet Roberts/Redferns. **Page 32** (t & br) Fin Costello/Redferns; (bl) George De Sota/Redferns. **Pages 34-5** (l & r) Fin Costello/Redferns; (m) Fin Costello/Redferns. **Pages 36-7** (t) Fin Costello/Redferns; (b) Richie Aaron/Redferns. **Page 38** Mick Hutson/Redferns. **Page 39** LFI. **Page 41** Fin Costello/Redferns. **Pages 42-3** Fin Costello/Redferns. **Pages 46-7** Fin Costello/Redferns. **Page 49** Ebet Roberts/Redferns. **Page 51** Richie Aaron/Redferns. **Page 52** (t) Richie Aaron/Redferns; (b) LFI. **Page 54** (t) Richie Aaron/Redferns; (b) Richie Aaron/Redferns. **Page 55** Fin Costello/Redferns. **Pages 56-7** (t) Fin Costello/Redferns; (b) Fin Costello/Redferns. **Page 58** Paul Bergen/Redferns. **Page 60** (t) LFI; (b) Steve Morley/Redferns. **Pages 62-3** Paul Canty/LFI. **Page 63** Fin Costello/Redferns. **Pages 64-5** (t) Janet Macoska/LFI; (b) LFI. **Page 65** LFI. **Page 67** Fin Costello/Redferns. **Page 68** Kevin Mazur/LFI. **Page 71** (t) Fin Costello/Redferns; (b) Fin Costello/Redferns. **Page 73** (t) LFI; (b) Janet Mocoska/LFI. **Page 75** (l) LFI; (r) LFI. **Page 76** Richie Aaron/Redferns. **Pages 78-9** (t) Steve Morley/Redferns; (b) Fin Costello/Redferns. **Page 80** Fin Costello/Redferns. **Page 83** LFI. **Page 84** Fin Costello/Redferns. **Page 85** Paul Bergen/Redferns. **Page 86** LFI. **Page 88** Fin Costello/Redferns. **Page 89** Fin Costello/Redferns. **Page 90** Steve Morley/Redferns. **Page 91** Steve Morley/Redferns. **Page 93** Ebet Roberts/Redferns. **Pages 94-95** Fin Costello/Redferns.

Every effort has been made to contact the copyright holders.
If any omissions do occur the publisher would be
delighted to give full credit in subsequent reprints and editions.